TRIFECTA

THE BUSINESS OF BETTING
THOROUGHBREDS FOR PROFIT

D1245887

BOBBY ZEN

outskirtspress

DENVER, COLORADO

Trifecta
The Business of Betting Thoroughbreds for Profit

Outskirts Press, Inc.
http://www.outskirtspress.com

ISBN: 978-1-4327-9119-3

Outskirts Press and the "OP" logo are trademarks belonging to Outskirts Press, Inc.

PRINTED IN THE UNITED STATES OF AMERICA

Reviews

I have been an avid thoroughbred fan ever since my Dad started taking me to the track at about age 9. I have been betting since about age 16, and a professional gambler for the past 10 years. I have read and enjoyed all of Bobby Zen's books. I regularly use his contender checklist. In his newest book "Trifecta - The Business of Betting Thoroughbreds for Profit" I especially liked the Money Management section. We all say we have the proper "discipline", but do we actually use it and track it? My answer was no to tracking. After Bobby Zen's insight to this I have set up a spreadsheet to do just that. So, thank you Bobby.

Calder Rick

Bobby Zen's Trifecta is a winning combination covering the most important aspects of handicapping thoroughbreds from selections to wagering. The astute reflections in his third book are sprinkled with humor and rightfully stress the importance of money management.

His advice is pertinent: "Work hard. Stay focused. Apply discipline." Ah, but horses are animals, he reminds us, and they can throw in "a clunker after running well the last several races. Look for excuses like a trouble line, blocked, steadied, etc. Was it the wrong distance, wrong racing surface, wrong class?"

One of his many essential observations hit home: "There is a quirk of human nature that we all have to a certain degree, a tendency to notice data that supports our point and ignore information that conflicts with it."

Remember what the great NFL coach Vince Lombardi said: "If winning isn't everything, why do they keep score?"

Greg Melikov
(Racing columnist Greg Melikov has
been writing about horses for decades.)

www.horsingaround.info

Bobby Zen's third book, Trifecta, is a solid one with a lot of information I have not seen before. The handicapping section is very good, with the checklists keeping it all pretty organized. I guess I've been guilty of the mental accounting that he talks about in here. The piece on risk analysis was an eye-opener for me; I know I can use that to help myself.

The lessons on discipline and learning to deal with losses and getting your head on straight, as well as not going bonkers when you win a few are great advice. For me, it's the kind of thing that makes you wonder why you haven't done that already.

The whole concept that is called handicapping yourself is also new to me, and worth a bunch on its own. It seems that I have a lot of things to work on, but I am sure this book will put me on the right track.

Tony Frieri
Founder of BSPT (Best Sports Picks Today)
sports and radio; Sports Expert

www.bestsportspickstoday.com

Books by Bobby Zen

Bet To Win!

Bobby Zen's Lucky 13

Trifecta

Author's note: Bet To Win! is recommended reading

Table of Contents

Acknowledgements

Bloodstock Research Information Services, also known as BrisNet, www.brisnet.com was a sister company to TSNHorse. Most of my references in Bet To Win! were to TSN which was absorbed by BrisNet. Most of the (TSN) products referenced remain the same or better at BrisNet, and all of the concepts from Bet To Win! are still viable and work with the products from BrisNet.

TwinSpires.com, a Churchill Downs company, partnered with BrisNet and also absorbed TSNBet, which was an ADW service I used and discussed in Bet To Win! TwinSpires does a wonderful job as an ADW with a lot of extra services thrown in. I highly recommend them, just as I did TSNBet.

Bloodstock Research Information Services publishes Track Stats each year (grouped by area and/or state), and are referenced in this book with permission from them.

Bloodstock Research Information Services also publishes Sire Stats each year; a most comprehensive guide profiling strengths and weaknesses in thousands of stallions. These play a big part in the AW section of this book, reproduced with permission from them.

Most of the racing statistics used are supplied by Equibase Company LLC, your official source for Thoroughbred Racing Information.

Thanks to Lisa, my better half, for her continued support as I toll through the trials and tribulations of researching and writing another book. I really did need to build the office in the garage!

Thanks to my brother, Fred, who has been a sounding board for me on this book as well as the original Bet To Win!

Thanks to Mac McBride, at Del Mar Thoroughbred Club, as I did extensive research on the synthetic racing surfaces. Mac provided good material and insights on this part of the project.

The horse jokes are some of my favorites that I have picked up over years of reading articles, magazines and stories on the internet. I did not write any of them and am not able to credit authors as they have been passed down numerous times. I hope they are a little reminder to have fun with racing.

Preface

This book is written to get much deeper into a few of the concepts of playing the ponies for fun and profit. My first book, Bet To Win! was written (in 2007) as an instruction manual to finding winners and covered several betting concepts. I stand by the process and continue to use it, with some revisions. Those revisions will be covered in this book, primarily in Part One.

The title, Trifecta, as catchy as it is, has substance; as the book is divided into three parts. Part One covers the picks, or handicapping information. Part Two covers the bets, including more money management, and how we make the betting decisions. Part Three covers the management end, including how to handicap yourself.

I received plenty of comments, good and bad about Bet To Win! One in particular stated that it was a fill-in-the-blanks system, which is absolutely not how it was intended. The Handicapping Checklist is devised to find contenders and apply handicapping concepts to make decisions about whether or not to bet, and best choices to make money if we do bet.

That is my intent with Trifecta, as well. I maintain a good presence on the web with www.bobbyzen.com, and still answer all emails and other communication personally. I love the game, and try to help others do the same. So, please, feel free to let me know if you like the book, hate the book, or just want to know who I like in the third at Delaware Park.

Part 1:

The Picks

1

Tools

The tools we are talking about here are the things we need to find live horses. There are a multitude of choices available for past performances, statistics, breeding, and other handicapping information.

The Daily Racing Form (drf.com) is the probably the oldest and best known to racing fans. They have a lot of good stuff, and have kept up with the information age as well as anyone. BrisNet (brisnet.com), which absorbed Thoroughbred Sports Network (a sister company) a few years ago, has state-of-the-art information in user friendly style. Equibase (equibase.com) also supplies solid information and stats.

There are plenty of other choices available in the search function on the internet, or you can go to my site, Everything Horse Racing (bobbyzen.com) and go to one of the links pages and find a Seattle Slew (ha ha, got that first joke under my belt) of sites available.

I use brisnet because they have the information in the format I am looking for that fits my handicapping style. Specifically, I use Ultimate Past Performances with Comments for this purpose. As we go through the handicapping process, references to past performances will be to this particular choice.

We use a Contender Checklist (see example) to compile our information as we handicap a race card, one race at a time. We also need the Handicapping Checklist (see example), which is really a 'cheat sheet' of sorts with most of the key information we will cover in this Picks section of the book. We also need a red and a black pen for filling out our Contender Checklist.

I can't help but think about the dozens of formats and concepts that I have seen people at the track use over the years. Now, I am *really* not knocking any of those choices, because if they work, by all means, continue to use them. But, I have seen Racing Forms so marked up that I could not read them. I've seen picks from the newspaper marked with every color in the rainbow. There have been Programs with hash marks, circles, squares and curse words scribbled on them. I have watched these various items get torn up, thrown down, swore at, and slammed against the wall in a fit of rage over the photo just lost, or the nag that ran dead last. Let me just say that I've *never* done any of these things. Have I told you about my short memory?

I just want to share with you a format that has worked successfully for me for many years. I remember a tip from Andy Beyer (one of my idols), talking about how the best players continually reevaluate their handicapping tools and make additions as necessary. I do that on an irregular basis, but I'm reviewing *everything* for this book.

There are many statistics that we will note as we go, and the main stat that we use for deciding if it is positive or negative, is the average size of a field, which is 9. That number in itself becomes a statistic, because if all things were equal, each horse in a 9 horse field has an 11% chance of winning (1 chance out of 9). I do use many abbreviations in my handicapping and simply mark the positive things in black, and the negative findings in red.

So, a statistic that is 11% or better for any particular horse gets written in black, as a good stat. A number that is 10% or less for any runner gets marked in red as a poor statistic. In short, any positive comment or finding will get written in black, and any negative comments or findings will get marked in red.

Easy, peasy!

Horse joke:

I had a near death experience that has changed me forever. The other day I went horseback riding. Everything was going fine until the horse started bouncing out of control. I tried with all my might to hang on, but was thrown off. Just when things could not possibly get worse, my foot gets caught in the stirrup. When this happened, I fell head first to the ground. My head continued to bounce harder as the horse did not stop or even slow down. Just as I was giving up hope and losing consciousness, the store manager came and unplugged it. Thank Goodness for heroes!

2

Prime Power

We use the Prime Power ratings from brisnet as our start point as we assemble our information for the Contender Checklist. We arbitrarily use the top 5 horses in ranking order, listing the top ranked horse first on the left. If he holds a 10 point advantage or more over the others, he gets a 55% in black. A 6 point advantage is worth 46%, 3 points 39%, and just being the top ranked horse is 31%.

I should tell you here that I listed full examples of all of the worksheets in Bet To Win and it would just be repetition to do them all again. I'm happy to send examples by snail-mail or e-mail for anyone that wants them, as my contact information is in the book. There are also quite detailed explanations of the Ultimate Past Performances, Prime Power and all of the other choices available at brisnet in their library function.

The four run-styles we use on the Checklist are E for early speed; E/P for early presser; P for off the pace runner; S for sustained deep closers. If there are numbers listed after the run-style it represents gate speed, the higher number being faster from the gate.

After listing the top 5 choices with run-styles and gate speed, you may already be able to spot a trend. The two most likely are only one front runner, or lots of early speed and only one closer. Depending on post position and track bias, this may have value. More to come on these concepts later.

A handicapping note here is that I run through all 20 steps on the Handicapping Checklist one race at a time. With practice, you should run through this process in an hour or two for an entire race card. I personally do not necessarily handicap each race, as I throw out some types of races I don't want to play.

Horse joke:

Three race horses stood in their stalls. One said to other others: "I ran 20 races and I won 15 of them!" he bragged. The next said with a snort, "Well, I ran 30 races and won 25 of them!" Then the third horse spoke up proudly, "Yeah, I ran 41 races and won 39 of them!" This seemed to settle the topic when the horses noticed a Greyhound outside their stalls. The Greyhound said, "I ran 100 races and I won 99 of them." The horses looked at each other in amazement and one gasped, "Wow! A talking greyhound!"

PRIME POWER

Contender Checklist

Results	Race #	Conditions	Dis	Prime 1	Prime 2	Prime 3	Prime 4	Prime 5
	1							
	2							
	3							
	4							
	5							
	6							
	7							
	8							
	9							
	10							
	11							
	12							

Bankroll						
Action Bets			Track Bias			
Win/place						

Handicapping Checklist

(Use black pen and red pen – red for 'bad')

1. PRIME POWER – BRIS rank   (3=39%, 6=46%, 10=55%)
   [Top 5]

2. RUN STYLE – E, EP, P, S with early speed number
   [E5]

3. CONDITIONS – List race conditions, look for the horse *most*
   qualified [Q]

4. LAST 3 SPEED RATINGS – Pattern up or down?
   [↑ ↓]

5. LAST 3 – Double or triple advantage?
   [DA – TA]

6. RACING SPEED AVERAGE – 5 Point advantage
   [RSA]

7. TRACK SPECIALIST – Won here (0-6), (1-10), (11% up)
   [(red) T] [T] [T]

8. DISTANCE SPECIALIST - (0-6), (1-10), (11% up)
   [(red) D] [D] [D]

9. TRAINER ANGLE – List the 'most applicable' angle
   [(red) 3%]   [25%]

10. JOCKEY ABILITY – Look for the 'most applicable' style %
    [(bad-red) J]   [(good-black) J]

USE Top 10 Qualifier list for contenders

11. CLASS RANK – Lowest level, past winning level, avg $ won,
    BRIS Class [$]

12. TRACK BIAS – Past week, meet to date
    [speed/closers/post]

12. A. Personal note; I do not play 'off' track conditions

13. POST POSITION - Compare to run style, distance, and/or last
    few races [pp]

14. WON LAST – Or number of wins in a row
    [w]

15. CLAIM – Last out or recent or multiple
    [C]

16. HEAD TO HEAD – Faced other runners/advantage
    [HH]

17. TIME OFF - Layoff, time between races, etc - over 45 days in red
    [265]

18. WORKOUTS – List as needed (Layoff, Maidens, etc)
    [w *]

19. WIN PERCENT – List as needed (Divide wins by starts) [25%]

20. BACK SPEED – Listed on BRIS

'Run' the race beforehand; who has advantages? What should happen?

Make notes during or after; what DID happen. Look for the chance to beat the favorite.

Note: If your top choice scratches, skip the race.

Handicap *Yourself*. What is working, what tracks do you win at, what type races work better, what surface. Play your strengths. Track your performance and document monthly.

Work hard. Stay focused. Apply discipline.

It's one long game, it's a marathon – not a sprint.

Have a positive, winning attitude. You are in it to ***win***.

www.BobbyZen.com   540-424-9992

bobbyzen@gmail.com

3

Conditions

I'll assume you have a working knowledge of the four basic conditions which are maidens, claiming, allowance and stakes races. I think one of the biggest points to reiterate on conditions involves reading and understanding the listed conditions for each race, *down to the letter.*

Let's review the subsets in each class:

Stakes races

G1 – This is the best there is, carrying huge purses, such as the Kentucky Derby with a purse of $2,000,000

G2 – The next level down, but still a very good race

G3 – One more step down (these top 3 are graded stakes, or black type stakes)

Other stakes will usually be named and will list the purse

Allowance races

These are listed as ALW, along with the purse size, and whatever specific conditions must be met to be entered in this race

Optional claiming races are considered an allowance type race, unless the horse is entered for a claiming price (again, written in the conditions)

Starter allowance races are allowance races where all of the entrants meet a condition that usually says they have been entered for a certain claiming price within a certain time-frame

Starter handicaps are similar, but weights are assigned by the Secretary or Track Handicapper

Claiming races

These are listed with the claiming price and any conditions that might be attached

Maiden races

MSW – The horse has never won and cannot be claimed

MC – The horse has never won and can be claimed for the amount listed

In the conditions, there can be dozens of variations that include age, weight, sex, state-bred only, to mention only a few. So, understanding these conditions is imperative in the handicapping process.

Consider the conditions as they relate to each horse as you go through this process. You may find a horse that barely qualifies for the conditions, and he would get a black Q, according to the Handicapping

Checklist. There may be one or more horses that should probably be entered in an easier spot, like a maiden racing against previous winners. This would receive a red Q, for not being properly qualified.

There is one tasty tidbit to look for, and that is a race that appears to have been written for a particular entry in a race. An example would be non-winners of two races since January 30, 2012, and there is one horse that won on January 29, won again between then and now, and ran a solid second in his last race! This happens more often than you might think! It doesn't make the horse a lock (actually, *nothing* ever does), but it sure gives him an advantage.

One other point in the class discussion is purse size as a good rule of thumb regarding class. Generally speaking, the bigger the purse, the better. The time this does not help you is shippers from one track to another, especially in this day of purses boosted by slots and casino money. So, a shipper from River Downs that ran in a $4000 claimer, with a purse of $3600; goes to Mountaineer to run in a $5000 claimer, with a purse of $8500. These are similar races, even though the purse at Mountaineer is 2.5 times greater than the purse at River.

Horse joke:

An out-of-towner accidentally drives his car into a deep ditch on the side of a country road. Luckily a farmer happened by with his big old horse named Benny. The man asked for help. The farmer said Benny could pull his car out. So he backed Benny up and hitched Benny to the man's car bumper.

Then he yelled, *"Pull, Nellie, pull."*

Benny didn't move. Then he yelled, *"Come on, pull Ranger."*

Still, Benny didn't move. Then he yelled really loud, *"Now pull, Fred, pull hard."*

Benny just stood.

Then the farmer nonchalantly said, *"Okay, Benny, pull."*

Benny pulled the car out of the ditch. The man was very appreciative but curious. He asked the farmer why he called his horse by the wrong name three times.

The farmer said, *"Oh, Benny is blind, and if he thought he was the only one pulling he wouldn't even try."*

4

Speed Ratings

We pull the speed ratings from the Ultimate Past Performances in two different ways. One is to look at them in the running lines of each horse, going back as far as ten races, if needed. The other way is from the Race Summary, which is usually more convenient.

Reading from left to right in the Race Summary are the four most recent figures, and we want to record any trends. If the numbers are going up, he receives a black arrow pointing up. This typically indicates improving form. Conversely, numbers going down receive a red arrow pointing down.

We also look for a Double Advantage; a horses last two speed ratings are higher than the last two of *all* other entrants. This one would receive a black DA on the Contender Checklist.

A triple advantage is treated the same way, but with a black TA. The triple advantage is a pretty strong sign that a horse will run faster than the rest of the field this time, also.

As we study the Race Summary, we look at the racing speed average (Rcg Spd Avg); here we are looking for a runner with a number that is five points higher than the next highest average. This indicates a distinct speed advantage over all the other runners and gets a black RSA.

Another high point from the Race Summary is the Back Speed, which gives us the best speed rating each horse has hit at this distance and surface. When we see a horse with improving speed figures, we know he might run back to that back speed number. If indicated, list this with a black BS (for back speed, not bulls***)! I know, 10,000 comedians out of work and I'm trying to be funny.

A strong angle that we don't see too often, is improving speed with a class drop. If we find this one, it gets a black arrow up and a black arrow down. One of my favorites, this one frequently points to the winner.

The Ultimate Past Performances list pars near the race conditions; these being par pace and speed numbers for this type of race. These give you numbers to compare to during the handicapping process, looking for runners that have at least matched this par number in the recent past.

A brief discussion of pace is warranted here. The basic concept being to identify the early pace (or front-runners) and the closers, or horses that will be coming from behind. There are pace figures, which are listed for the first call, second call and stretch run, all leading up to the speed rating. We want to decide if the pace of a race was an important factor in helping or hurting any horse in a race that was recently run.

Bris race shapes are also included in the Ultimate Past Performances, in the running lines with a 1c and 2c. These are typically positive numbers (for a faster than normal pace), or negative numbers (for a slower than normal pace). These can help decide how the pace will shape up in today's contest. The best angle here is usually an early speed horse that figures to get an easy lead. The other one to look for is the closer that will get a hotly contested early pace to run down.

The other way to analyze pace is the art over science concept, which involves looking at the run styles and history of each runner, and deciding how you think the race will be run regarding pace. This is one piece of the instructions listed on the Handicapping Checklist, which is to 'run' the race beforehand to try and figure what is going to happen during the course of the race. This concept, for me anyway, is the ultimate goal we are trying to achieve. If we get enough of these factors right, we land on the winner. If we manage our money right (more on this later), we cash winning tickets!

Horse joke:

What did one racehorse say to the other racehorse? The pace is familiar but I can't remember the mane.

5

Track, Distance and Racing Surface

There are a couple of points here that used to take tons of time and effort to get to the needed information. The questions being:

'How will this horse do on today's track? How will he do at today's distance?'

These are now simple to uncover by looking at the information box in the upper right corner of the past performances; it's all there in black and white. So, the runner that has won here before gets a black T (remember, *all* numbers must be at least 1 for 9, or the 11% ratio to be in black) on the Contender Checklist. Same goes for winning at today's distance, in fact, even underline the black D if he wins a good percentage of races at this distance. By the same token, poor ratios will get a red T or D accordingly.

These are huge angles that many players still do not even acknowledge, let alone using them as part of the handicapping process. But, what about the AW (All Weather) surfaces that many tracks have now? I despised these surfaces the first few years and admittedly, I'm still tentative about them. There is a line on the past performances to reflect the horses record on AW, and that's a starting place.

I did a lot of research (months, in fact) on the all weather surfaces and decided that some are playable, and that they are *definitely* not all the same. Here's a kind of rough and dirty review of my findings:

Track	Surface	Speed Bias Sprint	Speed Bias Route
Arlington	Polytrack	57%	53%
Del Mar	Polytrack	56%	43%
Golden Gate	Tapeta	64%	52%
Hollywood	Cushion	62%	61%
Keeneland	Polytrack	64%	60%
Presque Isle	Tapeta	67%	60%
Turfway	Polytrack	62%	55%

These statistics were gathered from Track Stats, by brisnet, and some end of season statistics pulled from Track Bias stats in Ultimate Past Performances (up to and including 2012). The speed bias considers horses with E or E/P running styles. It is easier to find a higher speed bias on most of the conventional dirt tracks, but many of the AW surfaces do not favor the closers as much as they did early in the life of the man-made surfaces. I think some of the better jockeys are learning how to ride more competitively on these surfaces, also. There are many trainers that still do not like (or simply will not) run their horses on the AW surface.

Since many of these tracks have had the AW surfaces in for several years now (going back to 2005), there is enough information to make better informed decisions than before. Trainer angles are now considered on switches from dirt to AW and vice versa, which also helps. One of the toughest angles is first time on AW, or first time on dirt. This presents the same dilemma as first on turf, as far as I'm concerned. Some handle the switch okay and some don't.

Fans of breeding can consider the Sire Stats, also published by brisnet, which has several ways to grade horses according to their sire. They recently added the category for the top synthetic sires based on wins over the Polytrack and Cushion surfaces. An A+ rating comes from a win percentage of 20% or higher, while an A rating represents 18% or higher wins. These are good numbers and become very useful in looking at horses making that switch to the AW track. The same concept applies to turf runners as they have a category for them, also.

I know I'm still stuck in my ways, in that I rarely make any serious bets on turf races or maiden races, but I will use them in a pic 3 or pic 4 sometimes. I definitely use the Sire Stats to help with my handicapping for these races, along with first runners on the AW surfaces.

Horse joke:

The Lone Ranger and Tonto walked into a bar and sat down to drink a beer. After a few minutes, a big tall cowboy walked in and said...

"Who owns the big white horse outside?"

The Lone Ranger stood up, hitched his gun belt, and said, *"I do... Why?"*

The cowboy looked at the Lone Ranger and said, *"I just thought you would like to know that your horse is about dead outside!"*

The Lone Ranger and Tonto rushed outside, and sure enough, Silver was ready to die from heat exhaustion. The Lone Ranger got the horse water, and soon, Silver was starting to feel a little better.

The Lone Ranger turned to Tonto and said, *"Tonto, I want you to run around Silver and see if you can create enough of a breeze to make him start to feel better."*

Tonto said, *"Sure, Kemosabe,"* and took off running circles around Silver.

Not able to do anything else but wait, the Lone Ranger returned to the bar to finish his drink.

A few minutes later, another cowboy struts into the bar and asks, *"Who owns that big white horse outside?"*

The Lone Ranger stands again, and claims, *"I do, what's wrong with him this time?"*

The cowboy looks him in the eye and says, *"Nothing, but you left your Injun runnin'."*

6

Trainers and Jockeys

This chapter covers the human factors as we try to ferret out the winners in these racing contests. I have them together because many of the statistics are similar, and one of the positive things we want to see are trainer/jockey combinations that win a high percent of the time.

Both of these folks have a tremendous effect on the horse; the trainer for everything leading up to the race, and the jockey on the track on race day. As a matter of fact, some jocks also work the horses in morning workouts, but you won't find that in the past performances.

There are many more angles and statistics to address with the trainer, not to mention the intent. He or she decides how often to work the horse, how often to race, at what level of competition, what strategy he would like the jock to use, and many other choices that must be made.

We get several key trainer statistics from the Ultimate Past Performances, including record for the meet, for the year and up to three stats pertaining to this particular race. There are dozens of choices here that might include allowance stats, AW to dirt, routes, sprint to route, shipper, 3rd off layoff, and so on. The decision here is which one is most pertinent to today's race. Now, we are back to art versus science, as you must have a 'feel' for which statistic to apply. I can tell you the ones I do not use, and those are small samplings (less than 10 races), as I don't think there is enough data to spot a trend.

So, having said that, we note the good numbers in black and the poor ones in red. There may not be any number written at all if there is nothing to get our attention. But, we are trying to figure out the trainer's intentions in this race. That is done with experience you might have with this trainer and/or this track. You can glean some of this information from the past performances, result charts, workouts, and other horses trained by this trainer.

Remember in the conditions discussion, we talked about a horse that barely qualifies for today's conditions being a good thing. That should be an indicator of the trainer's intentions, which are to win this race. Well, sure, aren't they all trying to win every race? Not really. If a horse has run last or near the back his last four times in a $7500 claimer, do you think he jumps up today to win for $12,500? Doubtful! When you really look at the past performances, including at least four or five key indicators, you should begin to get a feel for contenders versus horses just out for the exercise (racing into shape).

If we remember to keep asking the question 'What's he doing in today's race?' as we handicap, we should land on some winners. Applying that to the various choices the trainer has with horses should help us, providing we can answer with authority. What we are talking about here are trainer 'patterns', another angle that used to require so much research and homework to uncover. Many folks still do that homework, but if the sprint-to-route switch is pointed out as a 32% winning angle; what else do you need to know?

There are not as many stats and angles to consider when it comes to the jockey discussion. We get his (or her) win, place, show percentages for the meet and the year. The same info is there for horses with this run style, this trainer and this type of race (sprint or route).

Along with the obvious statistics, we look for switches to a rider better suited to this type of runner, or we note a switch to a rider *less* skilled at this running style as a negative. We might catch the 'hot' jockey getting the mount today, or the jockey/trainer combo that is winning a high percentage of races right now.

I do not downgrade a jockey with a low win percentage if he has shown the ability to win on this horse before, as shown in past performances or result charts. Otherwise, low percentage jocks probably continue to run low numbers. That will be at your expense, if you dare.

Horse joke:

There was a famous jockey that never lost a race. When asked how he achieved this, he replied, I whisper in the horse's ear:

Roses are red, violets are blue. Horses that lose are made into glue.

7

Class

Defining class in a thoroughbred is one of the toughest things to do in handicapping. Depending on who you talk to, there are several ways to do it. Some involve the pedigree, the price paid for the horse, the best level he is (or was) able to win at, just to mention a few of them. There are the 'canned' programs that brisnet and many of the other information companies supply. Which one to use becomes a personal preference combined with the amount of time you are willing to spend on this line item.

The class factor is handled systematically by me, usually relying on a horses performance in his last three or four races. I am looking for a level that he has been competitive, winning or very close to winning. I will consider that his current class and rank him accordingly. The Handicapping Checklist calls for a black $ symbol if he ranks better than today's level, and a red $ symbol for a lower level. Remember our review of the conditions to clarify this ranking.

Allowance races are fairly simple, using the purse levels as a guide. For graded stakes, I look for a horse that has won a graded stake and mark it as a G1, G2 or G3 as indicated. These high caliber animals are more likely to run back to a level they have been able to win at, unless they are obviously out of condition. This, of course, is why there are many factors in the handicapping game.

If I am using the brisnet Average Class Last 3, I am looking for a 2 point advantage over rivals. This is considered a substantial advantage, according to their library definition of this rating. So, those in a hurry, or not wanting to spend a lot of time on this line item, this is a good way to go.

What about horses moving up or down in class? That is a tough question, and there are several things to consider. Try to find what the trainer's record is with the 'up in class' or 'down in class' angle. If it is a significant number, it may be listed in the trainer stat's window in the Ultimate Past Performances. This is where I look first. The next place to look is the past ten races listed, to see if this has been done successfully in the past. After that, it gets tougher to uncover good information for this angle.

There are hundreds of scenarios with horses moving up or down in class, and I can offer some advice on a few here. Maiden claimers that have recently won can typically compete at about half that claiming value against winners. So, a winner for MC $10,000 might compete with $5,000 claimers, non-winners of two. Maiden Special Weight winner might compete against allowance runners (remember purse values). A $25,000 claimer that won at this level, ran okay against some tough allowance competitors, and drops back to the $25,000 claiming ranks is worth a look. A horse drops in to run against claimers for the first time in his life, is worth a look. Many handicappers are suspicious of horses with a big drop in claiming price. Is the owner/trainer willing to give up the horse; or is he glad to be rid of him for any price? These types are almost always hammered at the windows, so they usually offer no value to bettors.

Always understand the conditions of the race, as this is your first indicator of what a contender's class needs to look like. Remember to ask yourself, 'What's he doing in today's race?' to help decide whether he belongs here and whether he can win *this* race.

Horse joke:

A horse walks up to the bar and orders a drink from the bartender. The bartender sets the drink in front of him and says to the horse, 'Hey buddy, you can talk to me. Why the long face?'

8

Track Bias

The definition of track bias is a condition in or on the racing surface that will have a positive or negative effect on a horses run style. The first thing that comes to mind for many people is the weather, specifically rain and a muddy or sloppy track. This usually does create a bias, frequently with radical effects. But, there are many other types of track bias and we want to try and clarify some ways to handle this.

One thing to look at is the size of the track itself. This can range from five furlongs (5/8 of a mile) up to one and a half miles. Said in racing terms, this means a race at 1 1/8 miles would be a three turn race on the smaller track and a one turn race on the bigger track. Most past performances give a picture of the track with the start and finish shown for the race, so you can get a visual for this particular contest. Races starting near a turn are much different than the ones with a long straight run before the first turn.

We talked about the different surfaces in an earlier chapter; you should also know that a 'dirt' track might consist of sand, clay, loam or many other combinations. Many of the tracks in the western United States are typically harder (and faster) due to the different ground makeup.

Track maintenance might add water and then roll, till, and/or rake the surface with tractors pulling various equipment. Some tracks that race in the cold winter might add a type of antifreeze to the surface.

The temperature and humidity can have an effect on the racing surface. Any given track might typically favor early speed horses, or might hinder these types and favor the come from behind types. Knowing about a regular bias like this is a good starting point

You get that by being a regular at this track, or from the Track Bias Stats in the Ultimate Past Performances. The meet totals will give us the 'norm' for these multiple points of discussion. There is a ton of information here that includes the speed bias which is the percentage of races won by early speed. The impact values of all four types of runstyles, with the norm being 1.0, so the higher the number the better. The impact values for post positions are listed the same way, so we know the best post to be in. Another cool function here is a + sign, or a ++ sign by the most favorable runstyle and post position.

On our handicapping checklist, we are asked to 'run' the race beforehand. This track bias is a critical piece of that evaluation. Not only should we have an idea who should break best, who will make the early lead, who will make the big move in the stretch; we should be able to make a serious decision about whether there is a track bias *today*.

In other words, if the race plays out somewhat like we projected, there may not be a bias today. Remember that a bias means that something affected the horses ability to do what was expected of him. I usually want three or four races to make that assessment. This is definitely a judgment call; what if there is a huge speed bias and I miss two or three winners because I waited? That's me, after years of experience, being cautious. You might want to pull the trigger quickly, shoot first and ask questions later (I'm sure there's a joke in there somewhere).

Another point to consider regarding a track bias is making notes about a horse that performed well against a bias. Admittedly, this one is tough to keep up with, as it involves making those notes and tracking that horse for his next race. Several of the internet services including Twin Spires, Equibase, DRF and brisnet, offer results charts that you can read or download at your convenience. Many of the horse racing services offer a 'horses to watch' service that works well for this following these specific horses. Some websites, mine included, may even offer that list of horses to watch.

Horse joke:

A Department of Water Resources representative stops at a Montana ranch and talks with an old rancher. He tells the rancher, "I need to inspect your ranch for your water allocation." The old rancher says, "Okay, but don't go in that field over there. " The Water representative says, "Mister, I have the authority of the Federal Government with me. See this card? This card means I am can go WHEREVER I WISH on any agricultural land. No questions asked or answered. Have I made myself clear?" The old rancher nods politely and goes about his chores. Later, the old rancher hears loud screams and spies the Water Rep running for his life and close behind is the rancher's bull. The bull is gaining with every step. The Rep is clearly terrified, so the old rancher immediately throws down his tools, runs to the fence and yells "Your card! Show him your card!"

9

Tips, Tidbits, Points, Lore and Racing Lowdown

This is where I cover the rest of the items on the Handicapping Checklist, along with other stuff thrown in that includes everything but the kitchen sink (which is in need of repair).

A horse that won his last race, or multiple last races, is always worth a look. If he won last time, he is a threat again today. (Gets a black W).

Any animal claimed last out, or within the last couple of races, deserves a look. Remember, claims are for real dollars; they purchased the horse because they liked something about him. If there is a stat worth noting on this line item, it will be posted in one of those three listed under the trainer in the Ultimate Past Performances. (ex. 1st after claim 43%). Multiple recent claims enhance this detail even more. (Gets a black C or 2C for multiple claims).

Head to head competition is where a horse is competing against a foe that he has raced against in the past. If either of them finished in the top three of a prior race, they will be listed in bold letters in the top finishers of the past performance line. There are times when horses trade beating one another, but there are occasions where one animal gets the upper hand most if not all the time against an opponent. The upper hand gets a black HH; the one on the wrong end gets the red HH.

Here's a good current example involving the Triple Crown contenders of 2012. I'll Have Another (IHA) and Creative Cause (CC) raced against each other as two year olds in the G2 Best Pal, with CC mowing down IHA in the stretch. They raced each other as three olds first in the G1 Santa Anita Derby, ding donging it all the way down the stretch with IHA by a nose. In the G1 Kentucky Derby, IHA was much the best with CC getting a rough trip. They went again in the G1 Preakness, with CC finishing a distant third to strong running from IHA. I'll Have Another established the upper hand in head to head competition with Creative Cause, and CC's trainer, Bob Baffert, threw in the towel and did not run him in the Belmont. I'll Have Another was subsequently retired before the Belmont, but the point still stands.

Time off between races is a point of discussion among many handicappers. Although there is not a one-size-fits-all for this category, I do use a number here. Any horse off 45 days or more gets that number in red. Some horses can win off the long layoff, especially some of the higher class horses. Look at the past performances to see if this is indicated, or look for a good percentage from this trainer with layoffs.

This leads into the discussion about workouts. I do not put a lot of stock into workouts, but do look for them considering a horse with a layoff. I also look for them in maidens; in either case, I am looking for several workouts to prove that he is being 'conditioned' by the workouts.

As we work our way down the Handicapping Checklist, we see win percent listed as needed. This is kind of a tie-breaker for me, which I don't use very often. I might use it to pare down five or six contenders on one leg of a pic 3 or pic 4. It's basic math, dividing the number of wins by the starts this year (use last year if needed).

Once the information for a race has been entered on the checklist, you will typically see a lot of black notes and probably a lot of red ones. Something that only happens once in a while is that one contender has all black marks, while the rest are mostly red. This usually becomes your choice for this race, and is frequently an opportunity to beat the favorite. Otherwise, you are looking for the horse (or horses) with the most black notes, or some outstanding things that you uncovered during the process, or some of the highest percentages. These become your main contenders for betting purposes.

There is a handy function on the Ultimate Past Performances listed under the jockey and trainer statistics called the comment section. Points listed on the left are positive comments listed with a star, and points listed on the right with a bullet mark are negatives. These call attention to a something we might have missed during the handicapping process that might sway our opinion. Always be certain to note these comments.

The Key Race angle is another that is easier to come by than it used to be. In the old days, Steven Davidowitz, Andrew Beyer and other professionals like them had to dig this information out the hard way. The concept is that two or more horses from a given race come back to win their next start. Now, some of the information providers offer that info up; brisnet and Twin Spires handicapping view on the race viewing function are a couple that come to mind.

Here are a couple of points to consider when studying the line items on a horses past performances. Let's say he's been running well the last several races, but last out was a clunker, running last or near the back of the pack. When can we 'throw this race out' for consideration? Look for excuses like a trouble line, blocked, steadied, etc. Was it the wrong distance, wrong racing surface, wrong class? Or did he just not feel like running hard that day? This is an excellent time to remind ourselves that horses are living, breathing creatures. They are not machines, nor are they just numbers on paper. Anyway, the throw out race is a judgment call, and this is where the art part of handicapping comes into play. Sometimes it's an educated guess.

What about the 'bounce' concept? This is when a horse runs so hard in a race that he has nothing left the next time he runs. Sometimes this happens on back-to-back tough contests, sometimes after three hard races in a row. The pattern might show up after one good race in a lower class horses past performances; the point is to look for any pattern that might indicate a bounce. Another judgment call that probably gets better with experience.

HorsePlayerNow.com started a Night School in 2011 that is a very nice educational tool for the beginner or moderately experienced handicapper. It is well worth checking out and they offer pdf files of the material. Very handy.

I strongly recommend surfing the web for any info you can get in the horse racing field, or at least go to my site at www.bobbyzen.com (hint, hint).

Horse joke:

The husband of a blonde horseracing fanatic tells his wife, "You're losing all our money at the track. I can't stand it anymore. If you go to the track once more our marriage is finished." The blonde attempts to stay away from the racecourse for a week, and when the

craving becomes too strong she decides to go to a movie to distract herself. She's buys a ticket to a film about a girl who nurses an injured racehorse to health and enters it in a race as a long shot outsider. The horse is about to run in the final scene when the blonde turns to the man behind her and says, "I've got 50 bucks on the favorite." "You're on," says the guy behind her "I've got the long shot." Sure enough, the long shot beats the favorite to the finish. The blonde turns around to pay the man. I can't take it from you," the guy says. "I've seen the film before." "I've seen it, too," says the blonde, "but I figured he'd do better this time with the extra race under his belt."

Part 2:

The Bets

10

Money Management 101

The first rule in money management is discipline. This does not mean you scold your wallet and send it to bed early. What it means is being disciplined about how much is in your betting bankroll, preferably keeping that money separate from other funds. It means having a solid plan about how much you are going to bet, under what circumstances, and when you truly believe you can make a profit with this bet.

Great plan! Now, how do we do that? Let's get some basic stuff out of the way, then get into some pretty good details and concepts.

We got a couple of checklists earlier and we add one more here, called 'Betting is a Business' (see example). We are told to establish a morning line or odds chart. This is not easy as there is a science to it which looks like this:

A final morning line balances to 125 points. So how do we compute the odds to total 125 points? By dividing 100 percent by the odds plus 1, we arrive at a point system. For example, 2-1 represents 33 points (100 divided by two plus one). Odds of 7-2 are 22 points (100 divided by 7/2 plus 2/2 equals 100 divided by 9/2). Odds of 4-5 are 55 points (100 divided by 4/5 plus 5/5 equals 100 divided

by 9/5). By reverting to grade school mathematics, we multiply 100 X 5/9 to arrive at 55 points for 4-5. And we multiply 100 X 2/9 to arrive at 22 points for 7-2. Wow! I am a numbers guy and I don't like this math.

An easier way is to use this odds/points conversion chart:

ODDS	POINTS	ODDS	POINTS
30-1	2	5-2	28
20-1	4	2-1	33
15-1	6	9-5	35
12-1	7	8-5	38
10-1	9	3-2	40
8-1	11	7-5	41
6-1	14	6-5	45
5-1	16	1-1	50
9-2	18	4-5	55
4-1	20	3-5	62
7-2	22	2-5	71
3-1	21		

Okay, I don't do this for every race and you probably will not, either (accounting majors excluded). But, I do it for races that I plan to make a substantial (Prime) bet. The lesson is to understand what odds you should get in relation to the chance you decide your horse has to win the race. Like it or not, you need to do this to actually expect to make a profit betting horse races.

Action bets are different, usually involving multiple horses; for me, these are pic 3 and pic 4 exotics, where estimated payoffs are not possible before the last leg. For you, they might be exactas, trifectas, supefectas and whatever is the latest exotic to hit the program. The concept remains the same as we want the non-favorite to win in at least one leg to get a better payoff. You can get approximate payoffs for double and exactas with some services and tote boards, so learn to watch those.

A good rule of thumb is try to beat the favorite, but only when you feel good about your chances. You can't just arbitrarily bet against the favorite every time, but when your chances look good you can make some serious coin!

The bit about no impulse betting is sound advice. Trust me, I've been there many a time when I wanted to, or did, rush to the window at the last second because of (fill in your stupid reason here). Then there's always the guy that says "I *knew* he was going to win" after the race is over. He didn't know, and neither did you, or you would have made that bet earlier. Okay?

It's time here to run the disclaimer that I live by, and believe that anyone that gambles should also:

Never play with money that you cannot afford to lose. Not the rent money, grocery money, or any money that you know should be spent on something else. There's that discipline showing up again. Scared money does not win, and you will feel awful if you lose that money you needed for something else. It is great to win and a lot of fun, but not at all costs.

Betting is a Business

Bet *only* when you have an edge. Manage your money; maximize your advantage.

Odds Chart

Chance of winning	%	Approx. odds	Odds to bet win
> 50-50	50+	<1-1	7/5
50-50	50%	1/1	3/2
1-3	33%	2/1	3/1
1-4	25%	3/1	9/2
1-5	20%	4/1	6/1
1-6	18%	5/1	7/1
1-7	15%	6/1	8/1
1-8	12.5%	7/1	9/1
1-10	10%	9/1	11/1
<1-10	<9%	10/1	13/1

Set your own 'morning line', or chance of winning for all (at least contenders); this is your approximate odds. Be honest. Remember to handle your emotions.

Evaluate your bankroll before the day begins.

PRIME - Win/Place bets are up to 4% of bankroll. Watch pools for place bets.

ACTION - (exotics) are 5% of bankroll *per day*.

Pic 3 or Pic 4 qualifier: Should have at least one leg @ 39% or better win chance.

Play the overlay, avoid the underlay. (Easier said than done)

Beat the betting favorite when you can.

No impulse betting; no betting without handicapping.

www.BobbyZen.com   540-424-9922

bobbyzen@gmail.com

Another instruction on our Handicapping Checklist is to track your performance and document monthly. I believe that you must chart at least two statistics on yourself; your win percentage and won/loss numbers. You might be surprised at the number of people that lie to others (and themselves) about their prowess at the betting windows. Bragging is one thing, but you *must* know and face the truth about how well you are doing.

You can keep a simple ledger of some kind, or use the service that many of the betting sites offer. Twin Spires has one that works great; tracking types of bets, tracks, amounts and just about any time frame you want to work with. I not only track mine, but make them public annually on my site at www.bobbyzen.com.

Horse joke:

Young Chuck moved to Montana and bought a horse from a farmer for $100.00. The farmer agreed to deliver the horse the next day. The next Day he drove up and said, "Sorry, Son, but I have some bad news, The horse died."

Chuck replied, "Well, then just give me my money back."

The farmer said, "Can't do that. I went and spent it already."

Chuck said, "Ok, then, just bring me the dead horse."

The farmer asked, "What ya gonna do with him?"

Chuck said, "I'm going to raffle him off."

The farmer said, "You can't raffle off a dead horse!"

Chuck said, "Sure I can. Watch me. I just won't tell anybody he's dead."

A month later, the farmer met up with Chuck and asked, "What happened with that dead horse?"

Chuck said, "I raffled him off. I sold 500 tickets at two dollars a Piece and made a net profit of $898.00."

The farmer said, "Didn't anyone complain?"

Chuck said, "Just the guy who won. So I gave him his two dollars back."

Chuck grew up and now works for the government.

11

Money Management 102

Here is one of the toughest lessons for many gamblers to learn; as a matter of fact, some of them *never* learn this one.

You can't win them all.

Yes, you've heard this before. Not only can you not win them all, you should not play them all, either. Year in and year out, the favorites win about 35% of the time, and flat bets show a loss on favorites. A good handicapper should get in the range of 40% to 60% wins, so, the key is knowing when to bet and how much.

I follow a solid premise that has worked for me for the last several years and I learned it from two guys I refer to often, Andrew Beyer and Steven Davidowitz. It involves categorizing bets in one of two ways; Prime Bets and Action Bets.

Prime bets are win or win/place bets on a horse I think has a 50% or better chance of winning. Win odds need to be 7/5 or greater, and place money needs to be 20% or less of the place pool on your choice. As stated on the checklist, this amount can be up to 4% of my bankroll. This would be $40 if my bank was $1000.

Action bets would be 5% of my bank for the day, or $50 in any combination I want. This keeps me honest with the action bets, which for me are pic 3's and sometimes pic 4's. Why do I need to keep myself honest? In today's world of rolling pic3's, with a new one starting in every race sometimes, I could bet hundreds of dollars and not even *really* like any of them.

I use a percentage of bankroll because I subscribe to my own version of the Kelly Criterion. There are several books written on this and I have read many of them (some not exactly riveting). Long story short, if we bet a percentage, we can't lose all our money during a bad run. We increase bets when we are winning, and decrease bets when we are losing. I do not believe in luck, but I do believe in winning streaks and losing streaks (more on this later) and want to bet accordingly.

Okay, we have the amount to bet nailed down, and we need to decide when to bet. We've reviewed some pretty solid concepts here, with 'Betting is a Business', but there is a lot more to this aspect. This involves a couple of areas that do not have a lot of research reported, at least not what I have seen.

Let's refer to a book written by Gary Belsky and Thomas Gilovich called 'Why Smart People Make Big Money Mistakes', published by Simon and Schuster. They relay a story that many of us have heard about a guy betting $5 in slots and winning over and over, letting the winnings ride. He gets to millions of dollars and loses, returning to tell his bride that he lost $5. The idea being that he was playing with 'house money', or money that was not his. Wrong!! Any money you win is definitely your money, and should be treated as your money.

They are talking about a concept known as 'mental accounting', which refers to the inclination to categorize and handle money differently depending on where it comes from, where it's kept, or how it is spent.

Economic theory says that money is money; it's the same no matter where it comes from. The challenge being the varying emotions, discipline and willpower of individual people (note the d word again).

Credit card use can be a classic example of mental accounting. If we buy something for $100 and we had $200 in cash, we know we just spent half our money. If we make the same purchase with a credit card, we might not feel the pinch as much, even though our cost is *higher* because now we will pay back the $100 plus 15-25% interest on that same purchase.

Gary and Thomas tell another story about a girl that inherits $17,000 from her grandmother, who had scrimped and scraped her whole life to save this amount. Sara was afraid of losing Grandma's money in the stock market, so she stuck it in a bank earning 3% instead of a retirement fund earning 9%. This mental accounting cost her $16,000 that she could have earned in this particular saga.

They offer up the warning signs that you may be prone to mental accounting if ...

- You don't think of yourself as a reckless spender, but you do have trouble saving

- You have money saved in the bank *and* revolving balances on credit cards

- You are more likely to splurge with tax refunds or 'found' money than with savings

- You spend more when you use credit cards than when you spend cash

Why this discussion about mental accounting? I believe you must be able to 'reset the clock' after every wager, win or lose. If a large score or a large loss will send you reeling, be prepared to quit for the day and walk away. Seriously. If you hit three or four in a row and think you've suddenly got this game beat, brace yourself, because you do not. You are just as liable to lose twelve in a row at any given time.

If you find yourself down a lot of money (however much a lot means to *you*), and you find that you must 'get even', don't do it. Because not only will the amount bet probably be out of proportion, your handicapping now becomes jaded as you scramble for that bail out win.

Let's talk about a concept bandied about in the gambling world, known as the 'Gambler's Fallacy'. This is a belief that because there are certain probabilities expected in the long run, a short-term streak of bad luck is likely to change soon. It's why I do not believe in luck, because there is no momentum to change in random outcomes. But, here are some of the beliefs:

- A slot machine that hasn't hit in a while is due

- A poker player who has had several bad hands in a row is due for a good one

- A sports team with several losses in a row is due for a win

- Rolling dice and getting three 7s in a row is unlikely to occur a fourth time

- A roulette ball landing on red several times in a row will now land on black

The belief that there is a pendulum that swings back and forth to even these things out is absolutely not true. This problem with this mindset is that luck, as it applies to games of chance, is a series of *independent* events, with the next outcome unrelated to the last. So, if you think you are due to win, make sure it is based on solid handicapping, not because you lost six in a row.

One of the principles of behavioral economics, according to Gary and Thomas, is that people are "loss averse". The pain people feel from losing $100 is greater than the pleasure they experience from winning the same amount. Thus, that pain might make you do something crazy with your betting strategy.

I can tell you that on any given day, after four or five losses in a row, I usually pack up and go home. I know that , for whatever reason, what I am doing is not working on that day. "Live to fight another day" are words to survive by in the racing game.

Knowing when not to bet is as important as when to bet, and it is another aspect that many horseplayers struggle with. I know guys that say that they might be walking around lucky and not even know it! Well, I already said I don't believe in luck, and I would rather be walking around smart (no, let's say better informed). But, somebody's got to win the race, right? Yes, but I am not going to wager good money on the horse that might be the least slowest today!

I have several factors that I use when deciding to pass a race, learned over years of experience, many of them painful at the windows.

- I seldom play any maidens.

- I seldom play turf races.

- I seldom play an 'off' track.

- I do not play any race that I don't feel has a legitimate contender.

This is where the handicap yourself instruction comes into play. You must get a certain amount of experience under your belt, and track that information to begin to understand what your strengths are. They might be sprint races on dirt, route races on turf, maiden races at 7 furlongs, or any other combination of race types. The question becomes two-fold:

Which races do I win best at?

Which races are my worst ones?

Answer these and you begin to have a much better feel for when to bet.

Favorite quote:

"You were born to win, but to be a winner, you must plan to win, prepare to win, and expect to win."

— Zig Ziglar: Motivational author and speaker

12

Neuroeconomics

I said I would rather be walking around smart than lucky, which in this case means I have done solid handicapping and have what I think is a legitimate chance to make money with a wager.

What if we knew more, maybe a lot more, about how we make decisions regarding money? Recently, there have been a lot of studies on this subject. One of the definitions of neuroeconomics is the study of the brain in making economic decisions. Jason Zweig, editor of The Intelligent Investor, and author of 'Your Money & Your Brain', published by Simon and Schuster has some great insights on this subject. Most of his work is geared to the stock market; the spin to the race track is mine. (Isn't the race track the poor man's stock market?)

Jason recommends that we learn the basic lessons that have emerged from neuroeconomics:

- a monetary loss or gain is not just financial, but causes physical effects on the brain and body

- neural activity of someone making money on investments are similar to those of someone high on cocaine or morphine

- after two repetitions of a stimulus - like stock going up, or winning a bet - the brain automatically expects a third repetition

- once we conclude that returns are predictable, our brains alarm if the pattern is broken

- money losses are processed in the same part of the brain that responds to danger

- anticipating a gain, versus receiving it, are shown in different ways in the brain

- expectations of both good and bad events is frequently more intense than the actual experience

Understanding these lessons is very important to us as it relays to our decisions about betting. The part about getting 'high' on a winning bet is absolutely true; it's why many of us, self included, play the game. But, it's just as important to understand why these things happen, so we learn to make smart decisions.

We talk about trying to beat the favorite when we have a good chance of doing that, so explain your reasons why to someone (even to yourself, if no one else). Now, when you see me talking to myself at the track, you'll know why! It helps to talk out loud about why your choice looks better, just as it helps to review why another horse is vulnerable. Explain the bet the same way, in rational terms about why you are going to win money with this bet. If you can't do that, are you sure you want to make that bet?

There are many studies about dopamine, a chemical in the brain that helps us figure out how to take action that results in a reward. This is what gives us the high, or euphoric feeling when we get something that we really want. We also have a tendency to get used to a certain level, thus requiring a bigger hit (bigger reward, jackpot, etc) to experience the high again. Researchers also found that getting what you expect produces no kick. Hitting an unexpected gain fires the neurons, which is why winning big feels good (like a long shot or big exotic payoff). A third finding is if an expected reward does not materialize, the dopamine dries up (no fun).

Zweig suggests focusing on the things you can control which include:

- your expectations, by setting realistic goals for future performance based on the past (tracking your performance)

- your risk, by asking how much you might make versus how much you might lose (understanding the real odds versus your value odds)

- your readiness, by using a checklist (which we have)

- your own behavior, by stopping yourself before falling into any of the traps discussed earlier

Jason talks about a lot of similarities in the stock market game as compared to what (I think) we know about the racing game. Most investors expect their funds to consistently beat the S & P 500. Most investors overstate their performance in the stock market. Many investors claim they knew what was going to happen (after the fact, of course). The biggest challenge with this one is if you do that, you fail to learn from a mistake. The lesson here is that lying to yourself about how you handled a bet, does you no good.

People investing in the stock market get on a 'winning streak', making several good investments in a row, suddenly think they can't do anything wrong. Remember, like many kinds of repeating patterns, a hot streak makes your brain automatically expect more of the same. Sound familiar? Once you understand that monetary gains may have a narcotic power, you must learn to control it. Have fun, but don't go crazy!

We need to get an understanding of how much risk we are comfortable with, which is really the crux of this chapter. Not only is there no 'one size fits all' for this, but how much risk you can stand also depends on your current mood. Jason reviews several studies proving this somewhat odd finding (to me), showing that your "risk tolerance" can jump up or down on mood swings. Like a big loss, or several wins in a row, or cross words from your girl, or even spilling mustard on your shoe. Be advised!

Jason Zweig has a pretty good section on regret, including a scientific review of the insula, part of the upper brain. The insula is one of your brain's main centers for evaluating events that arouse negative emotions like pain, disgust and guilt - just what we feel when we lose money. This part of the brain is packed with neurons that help us adjust our behavior when things change. It also appears to be one of the places where your brain turns emotions into conscious feelings. So, when we lose money, these neurons fire up. Depending on each individual, this can be more or less painful, and will usually be relevant to the amount of money lost. This becomes a gauge for determining our risk tolerance and how we decide the betting challenge. I talked about my risk tolerance earlier; after four or five losses in a row, I am done for the day. You need to know what *yours* is.

I don't think it is too much of a stretch to keep a record of your mood as it relates to wins and losses. At least until you have a strong handle on not only your risk tolerance, but what happens to you after a big score, or several wins in a row, lost photo's, disqualifications, etc.

Favorite quote:

"Remember you will not always win. Some days, the most resourceful individual will taste defeat. But there is, in this case, always tomorrow - after you have done your best to achieve success today."

— Maxwell Maltz: was a motivational author
and creator of the Psycho-Cybernetics

13

How We Make Decisions

I know I am getting deep into an area that some readers are going to wonder about, but I feel strongly that these chapters on neuroscience and decision making are relevant to the betting game. I know it has helped my game, and I believe it can help most players, some even to a very large degree.

I read dozens of books on these subjects over the last few years, and not only saw many cross-references between books, but specific applications that can be applied to the betting concept. I have also read at least one hundred books on horse racing, handicapping, statistical analysis and similar subjects, without finding any of this cutting-edge information geared specifically to betting. So, if you are wobbling now, hold on to your hat when you get to Part 3!

One of these books was 'How We Decide' by Jonah Lehrer, published by First Mariner Books. He has written several books, along with editing and writing some blogs, and seems to be a pretty sharp guy. Early on in this book, he validates the discussion about dopamine. He also talks about how casinos learned to exploit our brain and the firing of those neurons that release the dopamine.

The short version of the casino exploitation (specifically slot machines) involves all the bells, whistles and flashing lights that sound on a regular basis. When you hit a jackpot, more bells and lights go off, causing those neurons to fire. Your brain tries to decipher the pattern that caused the dopamine to release (so you can get 'high' again), but the challenge is there is *no pattern*. Slots are entirely random, but your emotional brain will not want to realize that. There are thousands of slot machine fans that are going to want to argue, and I'm okay with that. The fact still remains that you cannot win money consistently on slots.

Enter the world of horse racing, and how we bet (and what happens when we win or lose). There are frequently patterns in racing that make complete sense, but there are just as many that do not. Like three races in a row won by grays, four races in a row won by female jockeys, five in a row by jockeys with green in their silks. We have already covered many of the positive and negative patterns in our handicapping section; just make sure your reasoning for your bets are based on sound decisions.

Jonah has a good section on the 'choke' concept, a dogma that most of us are familiar with. The idea is that a person or team that most believe should win or finish first in a contest or competition does *not* win, and possibly fails miserably. Performers call these failures choking, because they are so overwhelmed by pressure that they might as well not have any oxygen.

There are tons of examples in the world, and I am not going to list any here. You can think of some, I'm sure. The question is what causes it? There are lots of ideas about this, but it is actually triggered by a specific mental mistake: thinking too much. They usually start to focus on themselves, trying to make sure no mistakes are made. Actions are scrutinized that are usually performed on autopilot, and suddenly adjustments are made when none were needed. Choking is merely a vivid example of the havoc that can be caused by too much thought.

Now apply the choke concept to handicapping and betting on horse racing, and you can see what might happen if you over think what you are doing. This is another reason to have a solid handle on your strengths and weaknesses in this game, and stick to your guns. I know that I can usually identify the live horses in a race in about five or ten minutes. I also know that I am not going to make any last second bets, because of some sudden realization that I missed something. What if you are planning a huge bet on a particular race? Trick question; your bets should be consistent with your plan. I know if I spend another twenty or thirty minutes on the same race, I start to see things that aren't really there. I know what works for *me,* and you must understand what works for you.

Mr. Lehrer gets into some pretty good discussions about professional poker players and decision making. There appears to be an interesting parallel to my beliefs in handicapping, which is that there is a combination of science and art in both applications. The realization being that you can't just crunch numbers and statistics and come out a winner. This one aspect took me a very long time to realize; that you need to have enough information to identify the real contenders, and enough experience and gut feel to know when it is time to pull the trigger.

There is a quote from a particular guy, Michael Binger, who has done well on many occasions in the World Series of Poker, and is regarded as one of the best players on the professional circuit.

"What I love about poker, is that when you win, it's always for the same reason. You might lose because you got unlucky, but you never win because of luck. The only way to win is to make better decisions than everyone else at the table."

The relation to racing is very similar because you are, in fact, playing against the other bettors. When you win, it is their money, not the track's. The track gets their money up front. The lesson here is that if you don't think you have a decided advantage towards winning money in a particular race, then *pass the race*.

Just a couple of final points on this subject. One study shows that happy people are better at solving tough challenges, so, to be corny, I would say "don't worry, be happy." But, what I mean to say is to have fun playing the races. It should be fun and enjoyable!

The final point is from Jonah Lehrer, and it is:

The best way to make sure that you are using your brain properly is to study your brain at work, to listen to the argument inside your head. Remember when I said to explain your bet to someone (even if it's in your head to yourself)? Make sure that explanation is based on solid information and possibly some gut feel, which you will learn from experience how often gut feel works for you. We might even explore that gut feel later.

You are going to make mistakes, we all do. Become a student of error and learn from what went wrong. The next time you might just win that bet.

Favorite quote:

"Confidence is going after Moby Dick in a rowboat and taking the tartar sauce with you."

— Zig Ziglar: Motivational author and speaker

Part 3:

The Management

14

Handicap Yourself

I have been talking about this concept of handicap yourself for several years now; so what's the big deal? I spent decades in the business world as a manager and a pretty good leader, according to my colleagues. I have also spent years tweaking this concept of handicap yourself in the racing and betting game which includes managing myself. I know that I absolutely *do not* have it all figured out, but I'm sure this piece is as important to winning in this game as the third leg on a stool is. Bam!

Let's define this concept for the record. Handicap yourself means knowing and understanding what your strengths and weaknesses are in this business of betting thoroughbreds. It also means tracking and validating your performance, good or bad, on a regular basis. Finally, it means being smart enough to tweak and/or change your process accordingly.

These chapters on Management will intertwine my personal experience with some more excellent book references to give you the third leg of that stool that just might put you at the top of your game.

One of those books is 'Six Secrets of Successful Bettors', written by Frank R. Scatoni and Peter Thomas Fornatale, published by Daily Racing Form Press. This is a good read and is highly recommended. The basis of it you can guess from the title, and it covers interviews of various successful bettors. Here is the gist of the secrets:

1. They are entrepreneurs that make betting their business

2. They make the best of available resources and process information accordingly

3. They bet when they think they have an edge

4. They manage their money to make the most of it

5. They handicap themselves according to performance

6. They keep their emotions in check

These guys have a lot of concepts that are similar to my approach to the game. I would certainly want to use the phrase that 'Great minds think alike', which may be egotistical on my part, but, what the hay. Yes, there's a joke in there somewhere.

There is a pretty good review of the art and science of handicapping, another aspect that I talk about quite a bit. The art part consists of all the judgment concepts; the stuff that you might think is more or less important depending on personal experience. The science piece is easier, for me anyway; the statistics and records, the hard data you see in black and white.

To be successful at this game, you must be able to run this handicapping process on yourself. It means to take all the concepts and information that we covered in Part One and Part Two of this book, and figure out what works for *you*. If you have not been playing for a long time, at least a year or more, you may not be able to do this yet. Remember to keep track of your performance as we outlined earlier, so you can run your own statistics. I think you need at least one year's history to make intelligent assumptions for this basis.

If I was new to the game, or trying to learn this concept, I would like to see a checklist to walk me through the process. Here you go:

- What is my handicapping style?

- What class of race has my best win rate?

- What distances do I win with?

- What racing surface do I win more at?

- Which tracks do I win more at?

- Do I win more with certain jockeys?

- Do I have favorite trainers for my bets?

- Do I have solid past performances to work with?

- Do I have good track bias statistics?

- Do I win more with horses that look good to me in the post parade?

- What type of bets do I win more often?

- Do I track my performance at least monthly?

- Do I revise my betting and handicapping processes as needed?

- Do I keep my emotions in check?

- Do I manage my money properly?

This is by no means a complete list, but should get your mind working on questions you need to answer to handicap yourself. Once you go through this process, along with adding and tweaking to your specific wants and needs, you can say:

Yes, I handicap myself and know what works for me!

Favorite quote:

"I've failed over and over and over again in my life and that is why I succeed."

— Michael Jordan: is a former
professional basketball player

15

What You Need To Succeed

I made a reference to my experience in the business world as a successful manager. You do not need to have years and years of experience, or any experience for that matter, as a manager to be a winner in this business of betting. But, you do need to understand that you must manage yourself and your business of betting in a professional manner to expect to make a profit at it!

It is not coincidence that I hold an MBA, or that many of the books I refer to were written by folks much smarter than me, and some with more degrees than you can shake a stick at. The purpose of this book is to get this information out here for the betting folks to try and give them an edge.

One of those books is 'The House Advantage', written by Jeffrey Ma, and published by Palgrave Macmillan. Jeffrey was a member of the MIT Blackjack Team in the 1990's, and was the main character for the film '21'. He used math and statistics to master the game of blackjack, and reportedly made millions of dollars at it. His book conveys that information to the world of business, which is where we come in.

Jeffrey talks about the religion of statistics early on, with an experience at a casino where he lost six hands for a total of $100,000 in about ten minutes. Wow! If I'm honest, I don't know if I could stand that kind of hit. In his first year as a card counter, he had suffered losses, but nothing like this. He went back to his room to regroup and try and decide if he had played it properly, and concluded he did. He returned to play and won back the $100,000 plus $70,000 profit! He became a true believer in the religion of statistics.

There are several points to review on this strong belief in statistics, according to Mr. Ma. One of them is understanding variance, or runs of what we might call good or bad luck. Like we discussed earlier, several wins in a row do not make you invincible. A bunch of losses in a row don't necessarily mean you are doing anything wrong, either.

The point that follows makes sense in that you must keep a long-term perspective and remain confident in a proven system or method. Most successful analytic strategies will only give you a slight advantage, meaning you probably need to allow ample time to realize a profit. This is something that many, many gamblers struggle with.

So, the third point is that you need to be fully confident in your system or method, which is what enables you to stick with it for the long run. I learned this lesson the hard way, through long and painful bouts with various systems and angles over the years. I am embarrassed to say how many systems and books I bought in my struggling early years in this game. Some of these worked occasionally, none for very long.

Now, I am not saying that statistics are the be-all to end-all in winning bets at horse racing. They are a very important piece in the handicapping and the money management part of this equation, as well as understanding that scorecard on *yourself*.

The next part that we need to succeed is an understanding of something called confirmation bias. This is a quirk of human nature that we all have to a certain degree, a tendency to notice data that supports our point and ignore information that conflicts with it. Does anyone know a gambler that is superstitious, maybe even yourself? Better yet, know any gambler's that are not? Now's the time to admit it and put that demon to rest! You need to understand the dangers of decisions based on incomplete data. We talked about being honest with ourselves earlier in the book; when you screw up and miss a bet, make sure you understand what happened and whether you missed an important piece of information. Maybe it *was* a lousy ride by the jock, maybe you *did* get bumped down the stretch, maybe the DQ was *not* justified. But, then again, maybe you just don't want to admit the truth. Remember those famous and loud words: 'You can't handle the truth!' (We all recall Jack Nicholson here, right?)

So, avoiding this confirmation bias is not easy, because it seems to be built into our nature. But, it will be necessary for your success in this betting business. Jeffrey calls it thinking like a scientist, with the concept being that a scientist would not fall for confirmation bias. Their training and education would not allow it. Be a scientist!

I frequently refer to myself as a numbers man, using and understanding statistics in my handicapping and betting process. Early on, I fell into a trap that I think many handicappers do as far as numbers go. That is trying to reduce the process to a single number, getting all of the information you need down to that one magic number that points out the winner every time. Jeffrey Ma has a nice review of this same concept, recognizing it as an incredibly challenging task that usually does not work.

The difficulty lies in answering questions that have many variables that require subjective judgment, which is exactly what happens in the handicapping process. We want to use numbers (statistics) in our process, but stop short of looking for the 'home run' with a single number; I don't believe it exists. Many of today's handicapping processes available do reduce to a single number, including brisnet's Prime Power, which is part of my handicapping procedure. The key point being that it is a *part* of the process, not the whole ball of wax.

Reminder: A specific point on statistics is to make sure there is a good sampling. In other words, a trainer that is 0 for 3 at this track has a .0 percentage, but it is not a big enough sampling to throw him out yet. A horse that has not won at seven furlongs after four tries, does not necessarily hate the distance. I typically give the benefit of the doubt until there are at least ten numbers making up a percentage.

So, we know we need numbers/statistics to succeed. I also made reference in an earlier chapter about having enough information, experience and gut feel. So what about this gut feel? It's another area that Jeffrey Ma spent a lot of time on as it relates to business. His team used Coach Bill Walsh as an advisor to validate their results. They knew Walsh was a legend and a genius, but not so much of a statistics guy. What they found going through questions and answers with Coach was that his intuition was in line with their data-driven findings.

So, the question became whether there are (successful) people that make purely gut decisions, independent of any reasoning process? With a good review of this concept, Jeffrey comes to the conclusion that if you look at any successful person, whether in sports, gambling or business, data is at the core of their decision making process. I agree with that in horse race betting. I'm sure there are lots of bettors that play strictly on hunches and gut, but not so sure they are in that elite 3% to 5% that make money consistently with this style of play.

My point here is two-fold. That the gut feel concept is *part* of what we need to succeed, along with the other points in this chapter. The other is to use Coach Walsh in transition to the next chapter, about success and leadership.

Famous quote:

"I not only use all the brains that I have but all that I can borrow!" said Woodrow Wilson, the 28th President of the United States.

16

Leadership and Success

I link these two together because you need to view your handicapping and betting as a business requiring leadership and success. It is the concept I've been trying to build through this entire book. Even if your betting business is a one man show, you are still the leader, and it is important to think of it like that.

One of my favorite books on this topic is by Bill Walsh, with Steve Jamison and Craig Walsh, titled 'The Score Takes Care of Itself'. The book was published by the Penguin Group and brought to press in 2009, after Bill Walsh's death in 2007.

One of his concepts was that running a football franchise was like running any other business, which I certainly agree with. Bill was widely considered as one of the greatest coaches in the NFL, turning the San Francisco 49ers from a perennial loser to world champions three times in ten years. The story told in the book is of the ups and downs of creating this winning team, with a winning attitude, discipline (my d word again), and several other leadership qualities.

One of the first things he reviews in trying to find the path to success is learning about failure. No matter what information you have, what tools you are armed with, how well you think you are prepared, the road to victory usually goes through the place called failure.

Suffering a lot of defeats early in his career with the 49ers, he shared a list of do's and don'ts on the subject of getting beat.

Five things to do:

1. **You expect defeat.** If you are surprised when this happens, you are not a realist. This goes right with our betting concepts.

2. **You force yourself to stop looking back.** Review what happened, make adjustments as needed, move on. We said reset the clock earlier.

3. **You allow yourself recovery time.** A big loss or a tough beat can throw you off balance; allow the time *you* need, even if that is quitting for the rest of the day.

4. **You tell yourself "I will fight again".** This helps with the transition from the bad beat to clear your head, we said this earlier.

5. **You begin your next plan.** Focus on the fix, also helps the recovery.

These five things to do match up almost identical to concepts we have been reviewing in the betting business.

Five things we do not do:

1. You do not ask, "Why me?"

2. You do not expect sympathy.

3. You do not complain.

4. You do not keep accepting sympathy.

5. You do not blame others for the loss.

All of the five don'ts are likely to happen at the track after one, or perhaps several, losses. We've all seen it, probably even done it. Right? These are all things meant to help you get your head straight. It works.

Coach Walsh had an interesting perspective on looking back at a poor year, as far as a won/loss record. Progress, or lack of, can be measured in a variety of ways. He talked about having a keen eye and a strong stomach for digging through the ruins of a bad year. We need to do the same thing when we are suffering through those losing streaks that *will* come, they always do. Always analyze race and bet results to figure what was done right or wrong. Sometimes the way to kick that losing streak is to look closely; you may be missing some point or find a piece of information that you have been overlooking. Do anything to break a bad streak, *except* bet more! Stop betting and try to pick who is going to run last. Stop the bleeding!

Earlier, I told you my cut-off on any race day was four or five losses in a row. I don't throw in the towel forever and say I'm never going to play again. I acknowledge that what I am doing isn't working that day and pull the plug. I would *not* try to re-evaluate everything I am doing after that; I might after several losing days in a row. This is a little more of that gut feel that you must work out for yourself.

Coach Walsh had one of his lists (as you know by now, I believe strongly in lists) on habits to being a leader. I have pared it down some to fit our needs in the betting business:

1. **Be yourself.** You must mold your handicapping and betting style to your personality.

2. **Be committed to excellence.** Coach had a standard of performance that he was known for. Make sure you have high standards of what you will accept from your betting business.

3. **Be positive.** No reason to explain this one, is there?

4. **Be prepared.** Another concept we have been solidifying through this whole book.

5. **Be detail-oriented.** High performance is achieved with dedication to details. If you are not prepared to put in the work, don't expect to win consistently.

6. **Be organized.** Self explanatory. If you run your betting business shoddily, don't expect to win much.

The coach had an interesting perspective on managing confidence, on both ends of the spectrum, winning and losing. We have all probably seen people lose heart, lose faith, get angry and self-destruct after losing. But, what about after winning? Like winning the Super Bowl? Or winning the biggest bet of your life? There can be fallout after a big win, and the 49ers went through that after the first Super Bowl championship. Several players and members of the team were thrown off stride to varying degrees, many of them never recovering.

Being knocked off balance emotionally and mentally is a fundamental reason it is so difficult to continue winning, in sports and business. That team, with mostly the same personnel, lost twice as many games as they won the prior season. He called it Success Disease, and talked about the distractions and new assumptions associated with it. Heightened confidence, overconfidence, arrogance and the feeling that you've got it all figured out.

I still remember the longest run of winners I had in one day. I was at Tampa Bay Downs sometime in the 1980's, and my handicapping definitely left something to be desired. But, somehow I got on a run and hit seven consecutive winners and was, in fact, betting progressively. So, I increased my win bets after each victory until I got to the tenth race, which required a bet of about $60 to win. Understand that this was a ton of money to me at the time. You can probably already guess that I did not hit that race. More importantly, I spiraled into a losing streak that lasted a couple of weeks and spanned thirty or forty bets. No, I did not learn my lesson or know how to handle this. In fact, I began betting wildly and stupid and did cuss a lot while throwing my form against the wall! (Did I say I never did that? Did I say I had a short memory?)

The coach has a pretty good section on how to fix this Success Disease. When you reach this large goal or make it to the top, distractions and new assumptions can be overwhelming. It can make people relax their effort, focus, discipline and attention to detail that got them there. In our business, it can mean shortcutting the handicapping process or pushing vague amounts of cash through the windows on 'hunch' bets.

Some of the things the coach did to ward this off after learning the lesson the hard way:

- To allow the celebration and pats on the back for a short time.

- Make sure that you continue to follow the plan that got you there.

- Be demanding. Do not fall prey to this belief that getting to the top makes everything easy.

These should sound familiar; as they are similar to the rules and concepts we have been talking about in our betting business. Bill Walsh makes reference to mastery several times, stating that he did not believe there is true mastery. Instead, it is a process, not a destination.

He talked about Jerry Rice, one of the greatest receivers in NFL history, practicing slant patterns at 6 A.M. over and over with no one else around, to master his profession.

He talked about Joe Montana, one of the great quarterbacks in NFL history, in his last (15th) season as a pro, spending two hours a day on a practice field working on basic fundamentals.

Why? These guys understood mastery; that you never stop learning, perfecting, refining and molding your skills. You never stop depending on the fundamentals which are sustaining, maintaining and improving. These two guys, maybe the best ever at their positions, at the last stages of their careers were still working hard on fundamentals.

For Coach Walsh, there was no mystery to mastery. He certainly held himself to rigorous standards, constantly learning and trying to improve his game. It also applies to anyone who wants to get really good, to master a skill or profession. It applies to the betting business. It is also an introduction to the next chapter, where I push the edge of the envelope one more time.

Famous quote:

"The one piece of advice I can give you is, do what turns you on. Do something that if you had all the money in the world, you'd still be doing it. You've got to have a reason to jump out of bed in the morning."

— Warren Buffett: American investor and philanthropist

17

Mastery

I am not ashamed to admit I am a huge believer of mastery. I agree with Coach Walsh on it being a process, not a destination. I want to share just a little of my history here, if you will indulge me. I have a personal mission statement that is a big part of how I live my life, and I have been using this for many years. I revise it occasionally, probably every year or two, according to how things change in my life. It's also fair to tell you that gambling is not part of my mission; it is a profession/hobby that I make money at. I am not suggesting, or even hinting, that you *must* to do this to get your betting business working better. The point is that understanding the concept of mastery is a part of my mission statement, part of grasping the concept of continual learning, part of my process on trying to master this betting business.

Of course, by now, you expect me to tell you about the book I am going to refer to. I will not disappoint! The title is 'Mastery, The Keys To Long-Term Fulfillment', by George Leonard, published by Plume, a division of Penguin Books USA Inc.

I talked about my experience as a manager and a leader earlier. I used this book as a training tool for one of the last teams I worked with in Corporate America. It was well received and we had some accomplishments that I am still proud of today. Something else about this book; I have bought it several times. I have worn out two copies, loaned it out twice and never got it back, and distributed them as textbooks as mentioned earlier. Yeah, I like the book.

George does not give a specific definition of mastery, rather saying it resists definition but can be instantly recognized. That it comes in many varieties, but follows unchanging laws. Mastery brings rich rewards while not really being a goal or destination, but a process or *journey.* You need not be super talented or have gotten an early start. No, it is available to anyone that wants to get on this path and stay on it.

This journey can begin whenever you decide to learn a new skill, or hone one to reach for the top of a particular area. Mr. Leonard uses a tennis player as an example of wanting to get on the path to mastery for the sport. There are ups and downs, spurts of improvement, stretches of no gains at all, and the realization that it will most likely take a lot of work and dedication to master the game.

And so, the first piece of understanding mastery is that we never hit this point where we throw it on cruise control, we keep learning.

There is a discussion of three types of 'learners' that never quite get on this path to mastery.

- The Dabbler – Approaches each new challenge with great enthusiasm. New is fun. Quick progress is fun. The first plateau is unacceptable. On to the next challenge.

- The Obsessive – The bottom-line type, second best won't do.

Go hard, go fast. Applies himself to the maximum. Progress is good. The first plateau brings a doubling of effort, pushing himself mercilessly. There will be a drop-off, and it will be ugly.

- The Hacker – This one is willing to plod along without doing too much. Can go along like this until pushed somehow, then look for the next middle ground.

As you might guess, these types never really master anything. I know that I was a dabbler with all the books and programs as I tried to get a handle on this betting business early on. I have certainly been obsessive about getting this process down on many occasions through the years, to no avail. I have been handicapping and playing the horses for some forty years. Do I have it mastered? Of course not, but I think I'm on the path!

Okay, so what if there were some keys to this mastery stuff? Glad you asked. There are five.

1. Instruction – In the form of a teacher, books, films, audio programs, DVD's, computer learning programs, classroom, friends and associates.

2. Practice – For us, this is handicapping and 'mock betting' races, lots and lots of them. You will have plenty of time to play with real money after you get good.

3. Surrender - This can mean surrendering to the teacher, or to the demands of your discipline. It is tough learning a new skill, and you may have to give up on some or many of the ways you

have been doing things. Do not look for those 'Hit 90% of your bets with only 5 minutes work' claims here. See my earlier embarrassments for reference.

4. Intentionality - Several words describe this; character, willpower, attitude, visualization, and mental awareness. It is believing you will accomplish something; it is fuel for the journey.

5. Edge - Masters are dedicated to the fundamentals, *and* they take risks for better performance. They walk that fine line between endless practice and goals that do appear along the way.

The next point on the way to mastery is to understand there will be many plateaus, periods of time when no progress will be made. What is at first frustrating, becomes an enjoyable part of learning.

Another thing to discuss is something called homeostasis. This is a condition of equilibrium, or resistance to change, that is part of our human nature. This trait will work to keep things like they are even if they are not good. It's why bad habits are so hard to break, and why it is hard to start new (good) habits. What this means to us in the betting business is that whatever bad habits there are, they will be tough to break. Like betting the favorite heavily to win. Or waiting until zero minutes to post to make that bet. Or boxing five horses in the exacta when the payoffs are all low. You get the picture, fill in the bad habits that *you* will have to break.

Here are a few more things that you need for the journey towards mastery.

• Acknowledge negative things, but accentuate the positive.

- Set priorities.

- Make commitments and take action on them.

Watch for:

- Obsessive goal orientation.

- Laziness.

- Vanity.

- Inconsistency.

- Perfectionism.

A final note on mastery is one you may have heard before. It does not matter how old you are, what your level of education is, or your background; most of your potential is untapped. So, now is a great time to get on the path to mastery. By the way, I believe it *is* required to be on *top* of this betting business.

You may be wondering by now, besides questioning my sanity, why I would share all of this information. Why am I not concerned that all of my opportunities will be gobbled up? Simple math. For every one person that masters the game, there will always be ninety or more people that will continue to bet on names, numbers, colors and what have you. That's whose money we win!

I'll see you in the winner's circle!

Favorite quote:

"Discipline is the bridge between goals and accomplishment."

— Jim Rohn: was an American entrepreneur, author and motivational speaker

A Day At The Races

(Based on actual races July 5, 2012)

Bobby (BZ) has a friend named Billy (BA) that is an infrequent visitor at the track, and he asks Bobby if he can come along today. Bobby reluctantly agrees, but only if Billy follows the guidelines, as Bobby has been here before with his buddy.

Bobby has handicapped Delaware Park the night before and just needs to get the scratches. Billy has a printout with choices from a reputable internet provider of picks.

Race 1 is a claiming race for $7500 non-winners of 2 lifetime at 1 mile 70 yards. There is a pic 4 wager, and BZ has singled the 3 in this race, betting $24 in it. BA likes the 1, as it is the top choice on his sheet. The 3 is an early speed horse, has won at the track and distance, and is second off the layoff. The 1 is 1 for 43 lifetime, with a 3% trainer and comes from behind. BA plays the 1 $20 win and place. BZ explains that the 1 has a lot of red marks, and looks like a poor bet.

The 3 wrestles the lead from the 7 at the top of the stretch and holds off the 1 who is flying late. BA collects $30 for his place bet, claiming that he would have won had his jockey moved sooner. BA has his first beer.

Race 2 is a starter allowance for fillies and mares that have started for $10,000 claiming and never won 2. BZ was 4 deep in the pic 4 here as he could not split the contenders, with 1, 2, 4 and 6. BA played the top choice on his sheet for $20 win and place (which was the 1), who happens to be the favorite.

The 6 contends from the start and holds on gamely for the win at 7 to 1, the best odds of BZ's 4 choices. The 1 makes a run in the stretch and fades to fourth. BA is sure the 1 was blocked in the stretch but no one else saw it that way. He has another beer.

Race 3 is for claimers $6250 who have not won in 4 months. BZ is 2 deep in the third leg of the pic 4, with the 1 and the 7. BA lands on the 1 for win only at $20, as he half-listens to BZ explain that there will be poor payoffs on the 1 at .40 on the dollar. The 1 passes them easily in the stretch to win by daylight, paying $2.40 to win.

Coming into race 4, BZ has bet $24 and is alive with triple digit pay-offs on all 3 choices; 1, 4, and 7. BA has collected $54 against $100 bet. BA has already broken the bankroll rule, betting most of his $160 on the first 3 races. BZ had $60 to bet on action bets, which was 4% of his bankroll. He has not placed any win or place bets yet, as the odds have not justified a bet according to the chart 'Betting is a Business'. As BA heads for the next beer, he is reminded they are there to win some money, not get tipsy.

Race 4 is a $10,000 maiden claimer, and BA is going with the top choice on his sheet, the 7, who happens to be the favorite again, betting $10 win and place. BZ has cautioned him about playing the favorite most or all of the time, but race track habits die hard. The 1, who would have paid $244 in the pic 4, leads to the stretch and gets caught by a few, including the 4. This completes the pic 4 for BZ collecting $135, while the 7 finished at the back of the pack. Now BA wishes he had listened about the 7 never hitting the board on dirt, only turf. He does not want to hear that anybody can figure them out after the race is over.

Race 5 is a maiden special weight for two year olds. There are several first time starters, and after checking his Sire Stats book, BZ decides to pass the race. BA bets the 5 at $10 win and place on the 5, the top pick from the sheet. The 2 romps home a winner at 10 to 1, and the 5 is a game second , paying $3.20 to place.

Race 6 is a $10,000 claimer, non winners of 3 races lifetime, at 6 furlongs. Bobby and Billy both land on the 8, but with different bets. The odds are even money, making it a poor win bet for BZ, who keys him in the pic 3 with 1, 2 and 4 with 3, 8 and 9. This is an $18 investment with 3 choices in each of the next 2 legs, if the 8 can win. BA spends $15 win and place on the 8. The 8 wins convincingly, and BZ is into a pic 3, while BA collects his best hit of the day at $51.

Race 7 is another maiden special weight for two year olds, and BZ has no justified win bet. BA is on fire now (self-proclaimed) and bets $20 across the board on the 4. Yes, you guessed it, the top choice and the favorite. The 1 draws off and wires the field, while the 4 languishes near the back of the pack the entire race. BA has choice words for the jockey as he returns, and complains loudly for the next several minutes. BZ says nothing.

Race 8 is a $7500 claimer for fillies and mares, non-winners of two lifetime. BZ has 3 chances in this race, all with good payoffs. Since there is good money to be collected with a win in the last leg of the Pic 3, there is no justified win/place bet. BA has the top choice and favorite, the 3, at $.70 on the dollar, as he bets $20 to win. The 3 sets the pace for a half, and the 9 blows right by him in the stretch.

BZ collects $196 for the pic 3 (his picks ran 1, 2, 3) in this race, while BA comes up empty and angry.

Race 9 is an allowance race for non-winners of 2 lifetime at one mile. The 5 is an overwhelming choice on everyone's sheets, and at odds of $.20 on the dollar, cannot be bet by BZ. He does relax and gets something to eat, while BA can't wait to bet his last $30 to win on this sure thing. The 5 does win easily and returns $36 to BA, who has one more shot to make some money in race 10.

Race 10 is an Arabian race, and BZ stifles a laugh when BA says he has this one all figured out. BZ will not be betting the Arabians, so he is done for the day. There were only two bets made, and both were hit, collecting $331 against $42 wagered.

BZ's master plan is to hit the home run in race 10, boxing the 1, 2 and 7 in the exacta. He has $30 cash, which is just enough to bet the $5 exacta in the box. He did have the 1 and 7 running first and second down the stretch, but final finish was 4, 1 and 5. BZ literally cries as he sobs to Bobby that this was grocery money and he really needed to win today.

After giving him a vicious scolding about misuse of money, Bobby agrees to go home with him and try to explain what happened to his wife, but tells him he is going to have to be responsible. Bobby agrees to coach Billy one more time on his best chances to make money at the track. This will be next week, after the heat dies down a little.

A Lesson in Handicapping

Billy comes to Bobby's house as instructed, bringing a notebook with him and promising to wear his 'thinking cap'.

The lesson begins with the tools needed, which will be the past performances from brisnet (if you belong to TwinSpires, they are free with at least one bet placed). BA also needs a copy of the Contender Checklist, the Handicapping Checklist, and red and black pens. BZ explains the Prime Power numbers and what they mean, by showing the BRIS library, which contains explanations and examples of most of their products.

They review the conditions of a few races, while BZ explains the importance of understanding these conditions explicitly. They move through a review of speed ratings, and the various ways to use them. These include whether they are improving or declining, whether one horse holds a distinct speed advantage, and how they relate to tracks and distance. Bobby reminds Billy to make notes and numbers in black for positive points and red for negative.

The analysis continues with a discussion about trainers and jockeys, noting that there are many angles and styles to pick from in this process. BZ instructs BA to keep asking the question, 'What is he doing in today's race?' This can help with the ranking of the trainer if you can answer that question. The jockey aspect is a little more straight forward, looking for a rider that matches up to the horse and the needs for this race.

BA asks how to tell the class of the horses, and BZ explains that there are several ways to get to that one. BA wants the quickest way and the answer is to use the class ratings in the Ultimate Past Performances.

The next piece is the track bias and Billy is getting bogged down again on the details, which are covered fully in the 'Trifecta' book, so the default is the Track Bias Stats in the Ultimate Past Performances.

BA is quite anxious at this point and is reminded this whole process needs to be treated as a business, not a get-rich-quick scheme. Bobby sees this as the time to quit for the day, and Billy is given Chapter 9 as homework. It is fairly simple stuff that includes last race won, last out claims, head to head competition, time off, workouts, key races and comments. When he comes back next week, the review will begin with money management.

Money Management

Billy is surprised to hear that he must learn discipline to expect to make money in this game. Bobby asks him if he ever notices that BZ does not play every race? No, because BA is always too busy running around with last minute bets and grabbing another beer in between races. BZ tells him that is why I always do my handicapping ahead of time, and usually have many of my bets planned out pending scratches.

BZ hands him a copy of 'Betting Is A Business' and tells him that you must follow these guidelines to give yourself a fighting chance. BA is advised that he should have money set aside to gamble with, and that money should *never* be needed for any other purpose. That money is earmarked as the bankroll, and bets will be made as a percentage of that amount.

BA gets a nervous look about him when he is told that he should always want to beat the favorite (nervous because he likes to *bet* the favorite). BZ explains the part about avoiding the underlay, which makes Billy squirm even more.

Bobby tells Billy it is time to get to the tougher part of this training, which is evaluating what type of bettor BA is, and how well he does with managing himself. BZ already knows that BA gets reckless when he wins a race, or if he is betting with the 'track's money'. Bobby explains that any money won is now yours, and should be treated like you earned it the same as a paycheck. He also reviews the 'Gambler's Fallacy'; that you or a jockey or a horse are never 'due to win', because you have not won in a while. You make a bet because you can reason out why you think you will win, with solid information. Billy begins to get a little light-headed, as this does not go along with what he is used to.

BZ sees the challenge in BA's eyes and they stop the lesson and go for a soda. Not beer, but a soda or iced tea. As they are relaxing with a cool drink, BZ tells BA that he must get a handle on his emotions at the track. Sure, it is fun to win a bet, but it does not mean you are suddenly going to win several in a row. The same with a loss; they are going to happen and you must be able to put it behind you before you begin to think about your next bet.

Bobby asks Billy what type of races does he win more of, and BA cannot answer the question. He does not really know because he plays just about every race and has never kept track of this kind of thing. He guesses correct about needing to keep tabs on which types of races are more successful for him, but does not like the part about learning to pass a race if he does not *really* think that he has a good chance to win. He has to promise to track his betting on paper so he can get a handle on which type races are better for him.

Bobby tells Billy that he has some real homework to do before the next session. He needs to answer the questions in Chapter 14 of 'Trifecta', and there are fifteen of them. Yes, he must write down his answers.

When BA arrives the next week for the next review, he is uneasy about the homework he needed to do. Turns out that he was unable to properly answer almost all of the fifteen questions in the chapter. Bobby tells him that is okay, because you have to start somewhere. So, the teaching will be coming to a stop for the next several months.

Billy needs to keep track of all of the points that he could not answer, by tracking his performance, preferably by just making 'paper' bets (not using real money). He also needs to concentrate on the five Do's and Don'ts from chapter 16. Finally, he needs to decide how much money he can put aside for his bankroll when he gets ready to start betting again.

Billy wants to know about the Mastery chapter from the book, and Bobby just chuckles and tells him that will be a little further down the road. "See me when you have done all the things we have talked about so far, and we'll talk about getting you on the path to mastery!"

Bibliography

Belsky, Gary & Gilovich, Thomas, *Why Smart People Make Big Money Mistakes*, New York, NY, Simon & Schuster 2010

Lehrer, Jonah, *How We Decide*, New York, NY, First Mariner Books 2010

Leonard, George, *Mastery*, New York, NY, Penguin Group   1992

Ma, Jeffrey, *The House Advantage*, New York, NY, Palgrave Macmillan 2010

Scatoni, Frank R. & Fornatale, Peter Thomas, *Six Secrets Of Successful Bettors*, New York, NY, Daily Racing Form Press 2005

Walsh, Bill, *The Score Takes Care Of Itself*, New York, NY, Penguin Group 2010

Zen, Bobby, *Bet To Win!*, Denver, CO, Outskirts Press 2007

Zen, Bobby, *Bobby Zen's Lucky 13*, Montgomery, AL, E-Book Time, LLC 2009

Zweig, Jason, *Your Money & Your Brain*, New York, NY, Simon & Schuster Paperbacks 2007

CPSIA information can be obtained
at www.ICGtesting.com
Printed in the USA
BVOW06s1416071216
470048BV00009B/246/P